IDENTIFIED AS *Valuable*

Royal & Worth It

by

Renee Minor Johnson

*"However, you are chosen people, a royal priesthood, a
holy nation, people who belong to God. You were chosen to
tell about the excellent qualities of God, who called you out
of darkness into his marvelous light."*
1 Peter 2:9 (GW)

ISBN-13: **979-8218470760**

Published By:
Champions Within Kingdom Builders
Publishing Company

E-mail: championswithin2@yahoo.com
Website: www.reigningroyalty.org

TABLE OF CONTENTS

DEDICATION

I dedicate this book to my parents, Pastor Willie Minor Jr. and Orlena Minor (who both have gone to be with the Lord). They would proudly tell everyone they met that I'm a published author (especially my dad) if they were still alive today. I have two amazing big sisters who also believe in me, and they would agree with me in saying that our dad made us feel like we could accomplish anything we put our minds to. Although our dad is no longer with us, my sisters and I often encourage each other by repeating one of his phrases, "Yes, yes, yes... you can do it, girls... you can do it."

Daddy was one of the greatest cheerleaders ever! He would encourage anybody, anytime and anywhere. His affirming words reverberated over our family constantly. Daddy believed in tapping into the greatness inside of people. He was a true visionary with a vision for our family and for his community that was far beyond our understanding. If you were a singer, he would say, "Yes, yes, yes... you should try to get your songs on the radio." If you had the gift of reciting a poem or poetry with bold confidence, he would say..."Yes, yes, yes... You would be a great lawyer; you should go to law school." I've learned in my journey that words are seeds... and whatever word/ seeds you plant will grow. I guess that would mean that Daddy was a cheerleader and a farmer (smile).

Daddy was known for sowing seeds of encouragement wherever he went and with whomever he met. In 2002, when my husband and I developed Champions Within, Daddy began planting more seeds. He kept saying, "Yes, yes, yes... when are you going to write your book?" It took me a long time to believe that I had anything within me worth writing about. It was clear that I lacked confidence. I had to turn to God's Word and let Philippians 1:6 take root. I had to become confident that His Word was true, and He, who began a good work within me, will continue to help me grow in His grace until His purpose is fulfilled. I also had to speak "life-giving words. Remember this... words are seeds, and the seeds you plant will grow. That being said, it's always necessary for us to be intentional with our words. Why? Because words have power. Your future is listening.

Therefore, be purposeful and mindful to speak words of power and positivity to shape the person you desire to become.

"Live your life as a contributor more than a consumer." This quote from my father is one of the many pieces of wisdom he imparted to us. He always made us feel smart, encouraging us to be the best we could be and to give our best effort in whatever we put our hands to. Even when I didn't make the best decisions in life, his vision for my life never changed. One of his favorite Scriptures was Proverbs 3:5-6; he truly lived by it. Our father made a conscious effort to trust God and speak what he "believed to see" in us. This reminds me of the Scripture in Psalms 27:13 when David said, "I believe that I will see the goodness of the LORD in this world of the living."

I am deeply grateful for the parents God gave us and the solid foundation they laid for my sisters and me. Thanks, Dad and Mom, for teaching us how to trust God and run the race!

PREFACE

The quote, "Identity and Destiny are the valuably priceless pieces that fit into our preordained puzzle called life," encompasses a profound truth about purpose and existence. Here's an elaboration:

Knowing Who You Are

Identity is foundational—it is the "who" in the "why" of life. It encompasses your core essence, rooted in God's design. Without a clear understanding of identity, it becomes difficult to navigate life's complexities because identity acts as a compass. When you know who you are in Christ—beloved, chosen, redeemed—you can stand firm in your decisions, values, and purpose, even when life feels uncertain or chaotic. This understanding grounds us... giving clarity and confidence to move forward.

Divine Destiny is God's purpose for our life. According to Jeremiah 1:5, it's the reason you were formed in our mother's womb. The complete journey of our destiny route doesn't unfold in a single moment; it's a series of steps. The unveiling is often gradual as we walk in obedience by faith.

Understanding your identity aligns you with your destiny. It allows you to walk boldly toward the future God has planned.

Life is like a puzzle, with each piece playing a critical role. Some pieces represent joy, others pain; some are seasons of growth, and others are times of waiting. Identity and destiny are "priceless pieces" because the puzzle remains incomplete without them. They provide context and meaning to all the other pieces, helping you see the bigger picture—the one God preordained for you before the foundation of the world.

The phrase "valuably priceless" highlights that identity and destiny are not things you can earn or purchase. They are gifts from God, inherent to your design and purpose. No worldly achievement, recognition, or possession can replace their worth, as they are eternal and unchanging, unlike the temporary validation or material successes that the world provides. This divine value is not dependent on human standards or circumstances; it exists simply because God declares it to be so.

Practical Application

1. **Seek Your Identity in God:** Spend time in Scripture and prayer to affirm who God says you are.

2. Reject false labels or societal pressures that try to define you.

3. **Pursue Your Destiny Boldly:** Trust that God has a specific plan for your life, even if the path isn't always clear. Be faithful in small things, knowing they prepare you for greater purpose.

4. Trust the Process: Like a puzzle, life's pieces may not always fit... at first. Trust that God, the Master Creator, who is "All-Knowing," knows how to put it all together.

In summary, identity and destiny are not just aspects of life—they are the anchors and guides that shape our journey. These "valuably priceless pieces" ensure that every twist, turn, and moment fits into God's divine masterpiece for your life. As explored in the book Identified as Valuable, understanding your identity in Christ and aligning with your God-given destiny allows you to live with confidence, purpose, and fulfillment.

Our surrendered life is not about perfection; it's about following God's constant redirection, which leads us to become who we were designed to be. This truth reminds us that we are not random; we are intricately designed for a life of significance, where every puzzle piece has a purpose in God's grand design.

INTRODUCTION

Do you think you have value? Have you ever prayed while feeling unworthy because of what others said about you instead of what Jesus did for you? Think about that for a moment. Life is complicated, especially with various identities coming from social media and such. It can be hard to find our true selves among misunderstandings, social classes, religious beliefs, and ranking systems. The search for individuality becomes a challenging journey full of obstacles and uncertainties when done outside of our in-Christ identity. Yet, despite all the chaos, there is a clear divine revelation that goes beyond all earthly classifications and labels, solidifying who we are as believers in our in-Christ identity.

Welcome to "Identified as Valuable: Royal and Worth it," where we venture on a journey of self-discovery rooted in the unchanging truth of God's Word. In the eyes of the Creator, every soul is a masterpiece, intricately woven with purpose and divine intention. Regardless of societal standards or human judgments, each individual is valued as a very precious jewel in the Kingdom of God a radiant reflection of His boundless love and grace.

In the tapestry of humanity, every thread and every fragment is significantly essential. Each life and story contributes to the intricate design of God's plan. From the highest echelons of society to the humblest of dwellings, every person possesses ingrained worth and dignity and is cherished by the One who formed them in the secret places of the earth.

Even in our brokenness, even in the moments when we feel lost and alone, God sees us with eyes of compassion and understanding. He knows the depths of our hearts, the struggles we face, and the scars we carry. Yet, in His infinite mercy, He offers us redemption and restoration, transforming our broken spaces into sources of beauty and strength.

Let us embrace our identities as precious jewels in the Kingdom, shining brightly in the midst of darkness. We can walk confidently, knowing that we are known, valued, and deeply loved by the One who created us in His image. The written Word promises that we have been chosen as a royal priesthood and that we are a crown of greatness and honor. Join me on a journey of self-discovery and spiritual understanding, where we explore what it means to live a life identified as valuable, royal, and worth it.

Even broken diamonds still have value.

-Neyara Nior

CHAPTER ONE
A Diamond ... Is A Diamond

In our journey of self-discovery and empowerment, it's essential to understand that our value is not dictated by our circumstances or experiences. Just as a diamond retains its worth regardless of where it is found, we too maintain our value because God has declared it so. This chapter delves into the unwavering value we possess in God's eyes, emphasizing that our worth is intrinsic and divinely ordained.

Imagine finding a diamond buried in the mud. It is covered in dirt, unrecognizable, and seemingly worthless at first glance. Yet, despite its outward appearance, its true nature remains unchanged. The diamond's value is within itself, not its surroundings. Once cleaned and polished, its luster and worth are revealed for all to see.

Similarly, our lives can sometimes feel mired in mis-steps, or challenging circumstances that obscure our true value. We may feel unworthy, overlooked, or diminished by the trials we've faced. However, just as the diamond's essence remains untouched by the mud, our worth in God's eyes is constant and unwavering.

Our worth is not determined by our experiences or accomplishments. Instead, it is based on God's profound declaration about us. The Bible tells us: "For we are God's handiwork, created in Christ Jesus to do good works, which God prepared in advance for us to do (Ephesians 2:10." Our identity should come from the Creator, and if there is ever any doubt, refer to the manual... God's Word clearly unveils our value.

The Manufactuer's Manual

Have you ever purchased a new product and found yourself flipping through the pages of the accompanying manual, searching for guidance on how to operate it effectively? Whether it's a new gadget, appliance, or piece of equipment, the manufacturer's manual serves as a beacon of knowledge, offering essential instructions for optimal performance and maintenance.

Consider for a moment the significance of this manual. It is crafted by the very individuals who designed and created the product, individuals who possess an intimate understanding of its inner workings and capabilities. They provide the product with a name and purpose, detailing the steps required to unlock its full potential while also advising on how to avoid malfunctions or damage. This manual was created with the utmost care and precision, ensuring that those who follow it can trust in its guidance.

Just as a manufacturer provides a manual for their product, our Heavenly Father has given us a spiritual manual—the Bible. This sacred text acts as our GPS for life, offering wisdom and guidance to help us navigate the complexities of our existence. The Bible, like a manufacturer's manual, details the purpose of our creation and provides step-by-step instructions for living a fulfilling and purpose-driven life. It reveals our true identity as beloved children of God, created in His image and endowed with inherent worth and value. As we immerse ourselves in its pages, we discover the keys to unlocking our full potential and living in alignment with God's divine plan.

God, the ultimate Creator, has fashioned each of us with care and intention. In His eyes, we are His masterpiece... infused with inherent value and a unique calling. Our identity and worth are firmly anchored in Him, giving us a deep sense of security that transcends life's circumstances.

In the upcoming chapters of this book, we will explore the timeless truths found within God's Word. We will dig into the importance of embracing our true identity as royal heirs of God's kingdom and living according to His divine purpose for our lives. Through personal accounts, biblical insights, and practical wisdom, we will discover the keys to living a life of significance and fulfillment as identified throughout Scripture.

Embracing Whose We Are

When we look for our significance outside of God's Word, we often find ourselves wrestling with confusion and un-certainty. In times of difficulty or life changes, we may be tempted to seek answers from human wisdom or self-help resources. However, we often discover that they do not provide true fulfillment and purpose. As we conclude this chapter, we are reminded of the importance of anchoring ourselves in the Word of our Maker, the Manufacturer's Manual—the Bible.

In Jeremiah 1:5, God says, "Before I formed you in the womb, I knew you, before you were born, I set you apart; I appointed you as a prophet to the nations." This powerful statement reveals that our identity and purpose are not defined by earthly standards but by God's divine plan. Long before we face the challenges and doubts of this world, God has already been where we're going and has set us apart for a purpose.

The weight of this truth transforms how we view ourselves. It reminds us that our worth is not found in what others think of us or how we feel about ourselves, but in God's intentional design. Just as He appointed Jeremiah, He has uniquely shaped each of us for a special purpose. When we embrace this truth, we discover our true identity is rooted in God's eternal perspective, not this world's temporary opinions, agendas, or struggles.

For much of my life, I struggled with a lack of self-worth and low self-image, largely tied to my weight. The seed of insecurity was planted in my childhood, and for decades it grew, distorting how I saw myself. No matter how much weight I lost or how much external validation I received, I still saw myself through the lens of how others perceived me. Does that sound familiar? The warfare in my mind was relentless, and I was trapped in an identity crisis that seemed impossible to escape. However, things changed when I encountered the transforming power of God's Word and began to see myself the way He saw me. Slowly, I realized that my identity was not defined by my appearance, my past, or the opinions of others—it was rooted in who God said I was. That realization was the key that set me free from my mental prison.

"Your value doesn't decrease based on someone's inability to see your worth."
Zig Ziglar

As we live out our worth and recognize our ingrained value, we become empowered to live boldly and confidently. It is essential to refresh the pages of our minds and remind ourselves that we are not defined by our past mistakes, current struggles, or external perceptions. Instead, we stand firm in the truth that we are valuable because God says so. As we navigate life's hills and valleys, let us remember our unchanging worth in God's eyes. Much like a diamond emerging from the mud, our true brilliance shines through when we embrace our God-given identity and purpose, inspiring others to do the same.

In the words of Myles Munroe, "Your existence is the evidence that this generation needs something that your life contains." This profound statement highlights the truth that each of us carries a unique imprint to fulfill a specific purpose—one that was established before our existence. By understanding and embracing the guidance of our Creator, we can fully grasp our value and live out God's intent for our lives with confidence and clarity. I hope this chapter serves as a reminder of the incredible potential we possess as children of God. Our existence is not accidental but divinely orchestrated for such a time as this.

As we take a deeper dive into exploring our God-given identity in the following chapter, let us hold fast to the assurance that God has intricately woven purpose into the fabric of our being. With this understanding, let us journey forward with confidence, knowing that our lives are imbued with divine significance and that our actions have the power to shape the course of history.

~~~~~~~~~~~~~~~~~~~~~~~~~~~~~~~~~~~~~~

"Since you are precious and honored in my sight, and because I love you, I will give people in exchange for you, nations in exchange for your life."
Isaiah 43:4 (NIV)

"He predestined and lovingly planned for us to be adopted to Himself as [His own] children through Jesus Christ, in accordance with the kind intention and good pleasure of His will—"
Ephesians 1:5 (AMP)

For you created my inmost being;
you knit me together in my mother's womb.
14 I praise you because I am fearfully and wonderfully made;
your works are wonderful,
I know that full well.
15 My frame was not hidden from you
when I was made in the secret place,
when I was woven together in the depths of the earth.
16 Your eyes saw my unformed body;
all the days ordained for me were written in your book
before one of them came to be.
Psalm 139:13-16 (NIV)

Think about it:

What does it mean to truly know my worth and value in the eyes of my Creator? How can I align my beliefs with God's truth and step into the fullness of who He created me to be? Think about what it would look like to align your beliefs with God's truth. Let His love guide you forward as you embark on this journey of self-discovery and empowerment and lead you to embrace your true identity.

JOURNAL TAKEAWAYS

_____

_____

_____

_____

_____

_____

_____

_____

_____

_____

_____

_____

_____

_____

_____

_____

_____

_____

_____

_____

JOURNAL TAKEAWAYS

CHAPTER TWO
True Identity

Deep within us lies a profound sense of knowing—a certainty that transcends logic and reason. It's a gut feeling, an inner conviction that we often call "knowing within our knower." This innate sense of knowing is powerful. When we truly understand who we are and "Whose" we are... no-thing can shake us.

In our lives, we may draw our sense of "self " from various sources such as our name, family background, and accomplishments. While these may have a purpose, our true purpose comes from knowing our identity in Christ. Our spiritual foundation helps us understand our true purpose in life. It is important to realize that self-imposed expectations, worldly labels, and positions do not define us. Although earthly titles and positions may offer temporary validation; they are as unstable as quick sand. Seeking our identity outside of Christ inevitably leads to disappointment, for only in Him can we find true stability and security.

Our true foundation in Christ is unwavering and solid. It is not defined by external factors or fleeting accolades but by our eternal connection to the One who created us. As we delve deeper into understanding who we truly are, let us anchor ourselves in the unshakable truth of God's Word and embrace the profound meaning of our position in Christ.

Unveiling Our Spiritual DNA

As Christians, it is important to understand who we truly are. The Bible provides many verses that reveal our identity, and 2 Corinthians 1:22 is one of them. This verse is a beautiful reminder that our identity in Christ is sealed and secured. Just as an identification card confirms who we are in the world, the Holy Spirit within us serves as a divine mark of authentication—God's stamp of approval.

When we walk confidently in our true identity, transformation naturally follows. A transformed life reveals **"Whose"** we are through our responses to life's hills and valleys, serving as a powerful testament to our faith. Understanding who we are in Christ is the foundation of this transformation, and it is reflected in how we live.

To develop a relationship with God, we need to actively seek Him and receive impartation from Him. Through this relationship, we should begin to resemble Him and become more like Him. This is because we receive from those we're in a relationship with... be it good or bad.

People often vacillate between pleasing others and chasing material possessions because they lack knowledge of their true identity. A lack of understanding can lead to profound suffering. For years, I believed that people-pleasing would enhance my self-worth, but instead, it left me feeling drained and unfulfilled. Disappointment and disillusionment followed, and I found myself in a place of grief I had never experienced before. It took a minute, but I realized something profound; I was grieving something that I had never lost. The truth is, my royal position as a daughter of value was never taken away. Let that sink in for a moment.

When I was younger, my identity was closely connected with my parents. People would identify me as Mr. Minor's daughter or Pastor Minor's daughter. This made me realize the significance of strong relational ties. Our actions and characteristics are a reflection of where we come from, just like the fruit of a tree reveals its origin.

> "Define yourself radically as one beloved by God. This is the true self. Every other identity is an illusion."
> Brennan Manning

As born-again believers, we are representatives of God on earth. Accepting Jesus Christ as our Lord and Savior does not diminish our identity; rather, it reveals our true selves in Him. This revelation is crucial because our spiritual inheritance, which affirms our value and significance, depends on it. We are defined by who He says we are... nothing more and nothing less. In Christ, we are not limited by the constraints or labels that the world may impose on us.

Liberated Perception: A Renewed Self-Image

In the journey of self-discovery and spiritual growth, we eventually reach a pivotal moment: the moment of self-forgiveness. This is when we let go of the weight of past mistakes and missteps, freeing ourselves from the burden of guilt and shame. However, self-forgiveness is just the beginning; it marks the threshold of a profound transformation in how we view ourselves.

After self-forgiveness, a subtle but profound shift occurs in our self-perception. The lens through which we view ourselves begins to clear, revealing a new image—one liberated from the shadows of our past. No longer defined by our failures or shortcomings, we start to see ourselves through the lens of grace and redemption.

This transformation in self-perception is not merely a superficial change; it runs deep, penetrating the core of our being. It's a shift from self-condemnation to self-acceptance, from self-doubt to self-assurance. As we let go of the past, we make room for a new narrative—one filled with hope, possibility, and purpose.

With self-forgiveness as the catalyst, we embark on a journey of self-discovery—a journey to reclaim our true identity as beloved children of God. We no longer see ourselves as broken or unworthy but as cherished and valued beyond measure. This revelation reshapes our self-image, empowering us to embrace our inherent worth and potential.

As we embrace this new perception of ourselves... we begin to walk with confidence and authenticity. We no longer hide behind masks of insecurity or self-doubt, but step boldly into who we are created to be. Our interactions reflect this inner transformation, radiating grace, compassion, and humility.

However, this journey of self-discovery is not without its challenges. Old habits and thought patterns may resurface, tempting us to revert to our former ways of thinking. Yet, armed with the truth of our identity in Christ, we stand firm against these temptations, refusing to be shackled by our past. In the light of self-forgiveness, we see ourselves as God sees us—flawed yet deeply loved, broken yet beautifully redeemed.

Our self-perception is no longer distorted by the lies of the enemy but anchored in the unchanging truth of God's Word. And as we continue to walk in this truth, our liberated perception of ourselves becomes a beacon of hope and inspiration to those around us. For in Him, we find our true worth and purpose, and in Him, we discover the beauty of our creation.

Recognizing Our True Position

One of the greatest lessons I've learned in my walk with the Lord is this: what we do and who we are are two completely separate things. Jesus paid the ultimate price because He saw us as valuable. Our worth and identity are solidified in the shed blood of Jesus Christ. Do you find it challenging to separate the two?

I am the youngest of three girls; we were "daddy's girls." Since our parents have gone to be with the Lord, we often reminisce about how our dad would always try to make things happen for us. Each one of us could go to him with an attitude of expectancy. We were never afraid to ask our father for anything he had already promised us. We were confident of our position as "his girls." There was no second-guessing on whether he would or would not come to our rescue. My sisters and I embraced being "Willie Minor's" daughters with gladness, and when we stood in his presence, we stood in the posture of an heir... not an orphan. There is nothing like knowing who you belong to and what belongs to you.

In my mind's eye, I believe Daddy God wondered how long it would take me to come to Him with the same bold expectation I had with my natural dad. Realizing that my Heavenly Father had more stored up for me than my biological father could ever imagine my "God-fidence" (more confidence in God than man was born. That was the beginning of understanding my true identity. As wonderful as our earthly Father was, his love and provision could not compare to our Heavenly Father's. Knowing who we are in the natural (family lineage, etc. has "a purpose,"... but knowing who we are in Christ "gives us purpose." We are a work of art made new in Christ Jesus to do a work prepared for us beforehand. That sounds like we were created on purpose... for a purpose. Without recognizing the value of our identity, we live a life of compromise... settling for less than God's very best.

2 Corinthians 5:17 (GW) states that "Whoever is a believer in Christ is a new creation." This means that the old way of living has disappeared, making way for a new way of living. This new way of living involves rejecting the desires of the flesh and instead pursuing things that bring glory to God. As new creations who are walking in our true identity, we should strive to glorify God in all aspects of our lives. This doesn't mean that we won't face challenges, but it means that we will respond to them with faith and not fear.

In my desire to please God, I realized that when I approached Him in an undeserving stance, I was saying His sacrifice was not enough. That revelation alone caused me to adjust my posture to reflect my true identity. I no longer stand before God as an unworthy beggar. I stand as a loved, provided for, protected, victorious DAUGHTER... unafraid to claim the inheritance He has promised me. This shift in understanding changed my relationship with God, enabling me to approach Him with confidence and gratitude. It reminded me that my worth is not based on my actions but on His boundless grace and love. Embrac-ing this truth, I now walk in faith, knowing that I am empowered by His Spirit and destined for a purpose far greater than I could have imagined.

As we come to the end of this chapter, let us take a moment to reflect on the life-changing power of knowing our true identity in Christ. Let us embrace the reality that we are new creations, called to live a life that reflects the glory of God. With a renewed sense of purpose and passion, let us approach each day knowing that we are deeply loved and valued by our Heavenly Father. As we eagerly anticipate the journey ahead, let us continue to grow in our understanding of who we are in Christ and boldly proclaim His truth to the world. And remember, settling for less than our promised value is not an option.

Think about it:

Imagine the possibilities if we fully embraced our identity as beloved children of God and confidently walked in the truth of who He says we are. Think about how this shift in perspective could not only transform our lives but also impact the world around us. Keep these thoughts in mind and allow yourself the freedom to explore your true identity in Christ as you continue on your journey.

JOURNAL TAKEAWAYS

CHAPTER THREE

Faith to Reclaim Your Name

What does it mean to reclaim your name? In a world where external influences and societal pressures often shape our identities, the concept of reclaiming one's name carries significant meaning. It's about rediscovering our true selves as seen by our Creator and refusing to let anyone or anything else define us. As we explore this chapter, we begin a journey to reclaim our royal identity and embrace the fullness of God's purpose for our lives.

Through faith and revelation found in His Word, we'll learn to overcome fear, reject doubt, and confidently step into our destiny. Let's cast off insecurity and uncertainty and walk confidently in the knowledge that we are ROYAL —chosen, valued, and destined for greatness.

It's easy for us to have our identity stolen when we don't know God's Word, His promises, and His purpose for us. Fear has the power to distort our perception of our true purpose and bring our journey to a screeching halt. Fear and anxiety diminish our focus on God's ability to carry out His purpose through us. When fear takes root in our hearts, it blinds us to the truth of who we are in Christ, hindering us from stepping into the fullness of our identity as children of God. Fear robs us of the confidence and assurance we have in God's promises and leaves us vulnerable to the enemy's lies and schemes. However, God has not given us a spirit of fear but of power, love, and a sound mind. (2 Timothy 1:7) Knowing and standing on the truth of God's Word can help us overcome fear and reclaim our rightful identity as heirs of His kingdom.

In times of uncertainty and confusion, it's easy to forget who we are and **Whose** we are. But as we lean into God's promises and immerse ourselves in His Word, we begin to uncover the truth of our identity as sons and daughters of the Most High. Reclaiming our name is not just about rediscovering ourselves; it's about embracing the fullness of God's love and purpose for our lives. So, let's cast aside the doubts and fears that have held us captive and step boldly into the truth of who we were created to be.

The Bible tells us in Ephesians 6 that there is armor available to protect us against the schemes of the enemy. His tricks and traps are not blatant; they are very subtle. Satan wants to weaken our faith and leave us without a sense of purpose. The enemy is not after our job, car, or house; he wants to rob us of our faith. Jesus warned Peter that Satan wanted to sift him

> *"Failing faith weakens the pursuit of purpose... every time."*

as wheat, meaning he wanted to weaken Peter's faith. So, I'm here to warn you too: the enemy wants to weaken our faith and thwart our **"purposed" destiny**.

Speaking Life into Your Destiny

The first step to reclaiming our name with faith and living in alignment with our identity as God's children begins with being mindful of our words. The words we speak and the ones we allow into our lives have tremendous power, shaping our thoughts and ultimately influencing our destinies. Negative words sow seeds of doubt and negativity, while positive words cultivate hope and positivity. Therefore, it's crucial to be vigilant about what we allow into our minds and what we articulate, knowing that what we sow or permit to be sown will inevitably bear fruit.

If we want to change our environment, whether it's at work, home, or a hair salon, we can do so by speaking positive words into the atmosphere. However, we must also be careful not to allow negative words spoken in our environment to change us. Luke 6:45 (NLT) states that what we say comes from what is in our hearts. Our hearts are influenced by what we hear and see. Therefore, it's essential to listen to and watch things that align with God's Word if we want to possess His promises and speak His Word into our lives. Proverbs 18:21 reminds us that the power of life and death is in our tongues.

If we want to receive life, we must speak life. The power is in our tongues, and we will eat the fruit of our words... whether good or bad. Our future is listening to what we are speaking today.

Holding Firmly to Faith

Without a firm grasp on faith, our identity can become vulnerable to attack. Faith is defined as the unwavering confidence that our deepest desires will be realized and the absolute certainty that what we hope for is already waiting for us, even when it is not yet visible. As Hebrews 11:1 describes, it is the substance of things hoped for and the evidence of things not seen—a powerful force that instills fear in the hearts of our enemies. Glory, hallelujah!

So, hold on tight and don't let go! We must continue to stand firm in our declaration of faith, believing, as David did (Psalm 27:13), that we will see the goodness of the Lord in the land of the living. Remember, the One who made the promise is faithful, and He will surely bring it to pass.

Faith is the bridge between where you are today and your destiny. The revelation knowledge found in the Word of God builds your faith to fulfill your purpose. Faith comes by hearing, and hearing, and hearing, the Word of God. No Word... No Faith. Faithlessness can lead straight into an identity crisis. Holding Firmly to Faith is not just a mere act; it's a declaration of our royal lineage and a testament to our unwavering trust in the promises of God. As we stand firm in faith, we reclaim our true identity as heirs of His kingdom and boldly declare our allegiance to the King of kings.

As we conclude this chapter, let us remember that reclaiming our name is not just a one-time event—it's a journey of transformation and empowerment. It's about stepping into the fullness of who God created us to be and embracing our royal identity with confidence, boldness, and no compromise. Let us approach this next phase of our journey with faith and anticipation, knowing that our identity is securely rooted in Christ and that we are destined for greatness.

" *Reclaiming your name is not just discovering who you are, but having the faith to declare who you were meant to be.*"

Think about it:

As we reflect on the journey of reclaiming our name, consider the power of faith to reshape our identity and destiny. What would it look like if we approached each day with unwavering faith in God's promises and a steadfast commitment to our royal inheritance? How might our lives, relationships, and communities be transformed if we anchored ourselves in the truth of who we are in Christ? Take a moment to envision the possibilities that arise when we hold firmly to faith and boldly declare our identity as heirs of His kingdom.

JOURNAL TAKEAWAYS

"Boldly embrace who God created you to be, shedding the layers that no longer serve you or align with your divine purpose."

CHAPTER FOUR
Moving Forward:
Becoming the True You

Have you ever felt the pull to look back, even when you knew it was time to move forward?The narrative of Lot's wife serves as a cautionary account of the dangers of dwelling on the past and the importance of embracing our God-given identity. In Genesis 19:26, we read about the tragic moment when Lot's wife, unable to let go of her attachment to the sinful city of Sodom, looked back and was turned into a pillar of salt. This serves as a poignant reminder that clinging to the past can have dire consequences and hinder our ability to move forward into the future God has planned for us.

Jesus also reinforced this message in Luke 17:32-37, warning his disciples to remember Lot's wife and not to cling to what is behind them when the time for judgment comes. Those who are fixated on their past will be unable to fully embrace the new life and opportunities that God has in store for them. Instead of looking back with longing or regret, we are called to press forward in faith, trusting in God's provision and guidance for the journey ahead.

When we live in the past, we limit our potential and hinder our growth. It is impossible to grasp our God-given identity when we place more emphasis on what was rather than believing God for what is. Lot's wife serves as a cautionary example of the consequences of being unwilling to let go of the past and move forward in faith.

Moreover, holding onto past hurts, failures, or sins can cause us to forfeit the God-given inheritance that awaits us. Just as Lot's wife was unable to enter the promised land with her family due to her attachment to Sodom, we too risk missing out on the blessings and opportunities that God has prepared for us if we remain trapped in the past.

A lack of understanding our identity as God's beloved children can contribute to being frozen in the posture of our past. Failing to recognize our inherent value in God's eyes can lead to self-doubt, fear, and shame. However, when we fully grasp the truth of who we are in Christ, we are empowered to break free from the chains of our past and step into the abundant life that God has planned for us.

Understanding our value is instrumental in our ability to **live forward**. When we recognize that we are deeply loved and cherished by our Heavenly Father, we can confidently leave behind the things that weigh us down and focus on the prize that awaits us. As the apostle Paul writes in Philippians 3:13-14, "Brothers and sisters, I do not consider myself yet to have taken hold of it. But one thing I do: Forgetting what is behind and straining toward what is ahead, I press on toward the goal to win the prize for which God has called me heavenward in Christ Jesus."

When we let go of what lies behind and press forward in faith, we step into the abundant life God has prepared for us. In doing so, we break free from the chains of the past and fully embrace the future awaiting us in Christ.

Embracing Your True Identity

Have you ever felt the tug of uncertainty about who you truly are and where you belong? As we embark on this journey of unveiling our majesty, let's delve into the depths of our identity in Christ. Life's transitions may shake us, but our royal heritage remains steadfast. Are you ready to embrace the fullness of who you were created to be?

Life is a journey full of changes and transformations, from the very first moments of our existence until our last breath. However, despite the unpredictability of life, it is important to maintain a firm and secure understanding of our own identity. Without a clear sense of self-worth and value, we are at risk of experiencing an identity crisis.

One of my favorite movies, **"Identity Theft"** starring Melissa McCarthy, sheds light on this struggle. The protagonist, entangled in an identity theft ring, isn't driven by material gain but by a desperate search for inclusion and belonging. Her actions reflect a deeper longing to discover her own identity amid the chaos of her circumstances.

As the movie unfolds, it becomes evident that her criminal behavior stems from a profound sense of inadequacy and low self-esteem. Her desire for acceptance, rooted in childhood trauma and a lack of belonging, drives her to seek validation through illicit means. Despite the eventual revelation of her birth name, she remains adrift, lacking a sense of purpose.

While this story is fictional, its themes resonate with many real-life experiences. We often look to external factors to define our sense of self, whether it's our family name or societal expectations. Yet true fulfillment comes from knowing who we are in Christ, which gives us purpose and direction.

Identity Crisis

An identity crisis can occur at any time, causing us to question our sense of self and leaving us feeling uncertain and disoriented. It can be triggered by major life transitions, the pressure to meet societal expectations, or even moments of failure that challenge the image we've created of ourselves. These moments of inner turmoil can feel overwhelming, but they can also offer a unique opportunity for reflection and growth.

Whether we are navigating the challenges of adolescence, adjusting to a new season of life, or wrestling with un-expected twists and turns, an identity crisis often arises when our foundation is shaken. These experiences can leave us feeling lost and become pivotal turning points. Through faith and self-reflection, we can directly face these challenges and discover our true selves in Christ. This renewed perspective equips us to move forward with purpose and clarity, rooted in the unshakable truth of our divine worth.

As we conclude this chapter, let's take a moment to reflect on how life's transitions and uncertainties can shape our journey. I have personally experienced the challenge of navigating change. For years, I struggled to define who I was outside of my connection to my parents. Moving between different environments and schools often tempted me to adjust my identity to fit in or to shrink back in order to feel accepted. However, I have come to understand that our identity is not determined by the opinions of others or the settings we find ourselves in, but by the unchanging truth of who we are in Christ. When we remain steadfast in this truth, we can navigate life's changes with confidence and authenticity, embracing the person God created us to be without compromise.

Despite the challenges we face, there is hope. Our exploration of discovering our heavenly identity has unveiled a fundamental truth: our true worth and value are rooted in Christ. Our 'royal heritage' refers to the fact that we are children of the King, heirs to His kingdom, and therefore, we have inherent worth and value. This identity remains unwavering and secure, regardless of the changing circumstances in life. As we continue on this journey, let's boldly and confidently embrace the fullness of our created selves, uncovering the ingrained majesty within each of us. Recognize that our identity in Christ is the foundation of our strength and purpose.

As we turn the page to the next chapter, 'Dismantling Doubt,' let's prepare to dig deeper into the significance of preserving our identity amidst life's shifting tides. The shifting tides of life refer to the changes and challenges we face, such as transitions in relationships, career, health, or personal growth. With every change, may we hold fast to our pearls of wisdom and truth, knowing they guide us through the turbulent waters of change. This is not just about closing a chapter, but carrying its lessons forward into our everyday lives. Take a moment to reflect on your own journey of self-discovery and acknowledge the truth of your royal identity in Christ.

With renewed determination, step confidently into the next chapter of your life, knowing that your identity is secure and your purpose is clear. Let's commit to living each day with confidence, authenticity, and unwavering faith in the God who created us. Together, let's embark on this transformative journey, ready to unveil the majesty within us and shine brightly in the world around us.

Think About It:

Consider the opportunities that arise when you release past limitations and fully embrace your royal inheritance. How could understanding your true identity empower you to live a life filled with purpose and passion, even in uncertain times? Reflect on how letting go of the past can free you to pursue dreams and goals that resonate with your authentic self, and bring you a sense of fulfillment and joy.

Think about how this change in perspective could affect the decisions you make, the risks you take, and the strength you show in tough times. How might this clear sense of identity help you identify and seize the opportunities that come your way? As you ponder these questions, let them inspire you to move forward boldly, knowing that you have everything you need from God to fulfill your purpose and lead a significant life.

JOURNAL TAKEAWAYS

CHAPTER FIVE

Dismantling Doubt

Have you ever found yourself questioning what God says about you? What sparked that doubt, and how did it affect your sense of self? Doubt is a subtle and widespread adversary that first entered the human story in the Garden of Eden. In Genesis 3, we see the deceitful serpent subtly approaching Eve, not with a direct lie, but with a question that sowed seeds of doubt: "Did God really say...?" This seemingly innocent inquiry marked the beginning of a destructive unraveling as Eve began to question God's very words. The serpent's strategy was clear—plant a seed of doubt and watch it grow, distorting truth and under-mining trust. This destructive nature of doubt should urge us to address it with urgency.

This age-old strategy remains just as effective today. Doubt creeps into our minds, whispering lies that cause us to question our identity, value, and worth. One of the most profound ways this battle manifests in our modern world is through issues like gender dysphoria. This is one of the enemy's many attacks on our identity, causing deep confusion and pain as individuals struggle to reconcile their feelings with the truth of who God created them to be. Gender dysphoria, like other forms of doubt, strikes at the core of our understanding of ourselves, leading us to question the unchangeable truth of our identity in Christ.

Just as doubt was introduced by countering God's Word, it can be dismantled by affirming His truth. We can look to Jesus' example in Matthew 4, where He faced temptation and doubt directly from Satan. Each time Satan tried to sow doubt or twist the truth, Jesus responded with the Word of God, saying, It is written. Jesus' unwavering reliance on Scripture dismantled every attempt by Satan to cause doubt. In the same way, we must hold fast to what God has said about us—our identity as His beloved children, our worth as those made in His image, and our value as those redeemed by His Son. By doing so, we can dismantle the lies and stand firm in the truth, empowered by the immense power of God's Word.

Doubt is not just a fleeting feeling; it is a thief, subtly attempting to strip us of the ability to comprehend the true value of our identity. From the very beginning, the serpent used doubt as a tool to undermine the truth of who we are and what we possess in Christ. When we allow doubt to linger, it erodes our confidence and distorts our perception of the immeasurable worth that God has placed upon us. This thief seeks to rob us of the assurance that we are fearfully and wonderfully made, chosen, and deeply loved by our Creator.

Remember, the serpent aimed to make Eve doubt her position and relationship with God. Yet, we are called to reclaim and reinforce that position, knowing that God's Word is unchanging and His love for us is unwavering. This unchanging truth is a source of security and love we can always rely on. The empowering nature of God's Word should instill in you a profound sense of security and peace, even in the face of doubt.

When we dismantle doubt, we are defending ourselves against its corrosive effects and reclaiming the fullness of our identity in Christ. We must be vigilant, understanding that doubt will rise up, especially in times of transition or uncertainty, aiming to shake our faith and make us question our value. However, by grounding ourselves in God's unchanging truth, we can stand firm, fully compre-hending and embracing the identity that has been gifted to us by our Heavenly Father. This process is not just a passive acceptance but an active reclaiming of our true identity. It is the key to navigating life's challenges with confidence and purpose. In this space, we know without a doubt who we are and Whose we are.

Maneuvering the Tilts and Turns

In life's transitions, doubt resurfaces with greater in-tensity when we are most vulnerable and uncertain. In these critical moments—the turns and twists of our journey —doubt can gain a stronghold if we're not vigilant. This is why we must deal with doubt urgently and decisively. If we allow it to linger, it will grow stronger, complicating our ability to navigate the transitions that require our faith to be steadfast. Let us be proactive in confronting doubt, grounding ourselves in the truth of God's Word so that when the inevitable turns come, we are anchored in our true identity, unshaken and resolute in our purpose.

As we maneuver the swift currents of life, let us cling firmly to our identity. By doing so, we can weather any storm, emerge from any transition, and remain steadfast in the truth of who we are and WHOSE we are. Who we are in Christ is our most valuable asset, a treasure to be cherished and protected. So... let us protect it with the same vigilance as our most treasured gems.

Viewing transitions as chances to build our faith allows us to arise stronger and more confident in our position rather than our condition. Our position as a child of God remains steadfast, regardless of our circumstances. Reflecting on past experiences can offer valuable insights and help us handle future changes more effectively when viewed through the lens of God's promises. Ultimately, by holding tight in the turns, we embrace our core values and confidently navigate transitions. We also grow in grace, trusting in who God says we are.

We may face uncertainty in many areas of life, but understanding the value of our identity should never be one of them. Our identity is at the core of our being—a precious gem defining who we are and whose we are. It shapes our actions, decisions, and ultimately, our destiny. In a world constantly bombarding us with shifting norms and trends, it is now more crucial than ever to dismantle doubt, deepen our understanding of ourselves, and embrace our true value.

As we dismantle doubt, we uncover a clearer view of our true worth. Just as adjusting a gem scope brings a diamond's brilliance into focus, changing our perspective to align with God's truth allows us to see the full value of our identity. In the next section, we will explore how this process of realignment fosters an internal transformation. This inner shift... empowers us to navigate and maneuver life's transitions with renewed purpose and unwavering confidence.

Transformational Realization

Once doubt is dismantled, it opens the way for a clearer view. It's like adjusting the lens on a gem scope or camera—when the blurriness is removed, the true brilliance of the gem is revealed. In the same way, as we dismantle doubt, we begin to see ourselves as God sees us, with clarity and precision.

Imagine viewing a precious stone through a gem scope. Initially, the gem may appear dull or flawed, but as you carefully adjust the lens, its true value and intricate de-tails come into focus. This is much like the journey of recognizing our worth in Christ. The enemy's lies can cloud our vision, making us doubt our value. However, as we continually adjust our perspective—realigning it with God's truth—the doubts fade, and the beauty of our identity in Christ becomes unmistakably clear.

If I had a dollar for every time I've had to readjust my lens to disregard the enemy's lies, I would be on my way to millionaire status! What am I saying? I'm saying that tearing down doubt is not an easy feat—it's a day-by-day, piece-by-piece process. Each time we adjust our lens, we better understand our worth and purpose. This ongoing process leads to a transformational realization: the more we align our perspective with God's truth, the more we embrace the fullness of who we are in Him.

Just as a jeweler meticulously examines and values each facet of a gem, God sees every part of us with the utmost care and value. By continually adjusting our lens to see ourselves through His eyes, we can fully grasp our true identity and worth, leading to a life of purpose and fulfillment.

In the next chapter, we will explore how recognizing our inherent worth and validation in God's eyes enables us to face life's changes with confidence and purpose. Let's delve into the truth that our Heavenly Father sees immeasurable value in us. This realization will enhance our ability to navigate life's inevitable transitions with self-assurance and grace.

Think About It:

What modern-day tactics make you question your value and worth? Is it societal pressure, comparison on social media, or personal failures? Identify any lingering doubts about your identity and bring them before God, asking Him to replace them with His truth.

Guard your mind against these attacks by following Jesus' example in Matthew 4—use God's Word to dismantle doubt and affirm your identity in Christ. Doubt is a destructive force that can distort your sense of self, so addressing it urgently is crucial.

As you clear away doubt, your true worth becomes more visible, like adjusting a lens to see a diamond's brilliance. How will you respond to this clarity, and how will you apply it in your daily life? Let God's Word be your constant source of guidance and reassurance as you navigate life with confidence.

"Change is inevitable, but GROWTH is optional."

John C. Maxwell

JOURNAL TAKEAWAYS

_____

_____

_____

_____

_____

_____

_____

_____

_____

_____

_____

_____

_____

_____

_____

_____

MY WORTH IS...

My worth is beyond worldly bells and whistles and deceptive lies that the enemy whispers.

My worth is above the circumstances I see, and the illusional barriers designed to break me...

My worth is much louder than the voices on-blast, attempting to keep me attached to my past...

My worth is greater than the world's glitz and glimmer with a short-lived shine that gets dimmer and dimmer.

My value is appraised by the life that was given, and the blood that was shed which gives me permission- to dream... to build... to fail... and succeed.

My worth is in Christ... my Savior indeed!

"The price He paid confirms our value!"

CHAPTER SIX
Valued and Validated

For many years, I have been pondering on the question, "How does God see me?" However, I struggled to grasp His perspective. It took me a lot of time to realize that God sees me as His beloved daughter. Despite my understanding of God as majestic and powerful, I failed to comprehend His role as a loving Father, as described in Galatians 4:6. My perception of myself greatly influenced how I viewed our Heavenly Father.

In simple terms, I saw God as the employer and myself as an employee. I lacked awareness of my identity as an heir to His kingdom. I was oblivious to the rights and privileges bestowed upon me as His daughter. This skewed perception hindered my ability to fully embrace my value and worth through God's eyes.

And because we are his children, God has sent the
Spirit of his Son into our hearts, prompting
us to call out, "Abba, Father".
Galatians 4:6 (NLT)

My husband and I have a blended family comprised of four boys and one girl. I like to refer to it as "a family of one" - many members, one family. When we first met, I was a single parent to my eight-year-old son. Remarkably, just a few months after meeting, my husband expressed his desire to adopt my son. He wanted my son to bear his last name and enjoy all the privileges and benefits that came with it. Right from the start, my husband embraced my son as his own, treating him with love and care in every aspect - physically, emotionally, financially, and spiritually... and I reciprocated the same to his children as well.

In much the same way, our spiritual adoption into the family of God comes with a multitude of benefits. Just as someone who is adopted into a loving family gains all the privileges and rights of belonging to that family, we, as children of God, are granted access to an unparalleled spiritual benefits package. Our position as children of the **Most High** grants us immediate access to every spiritual blessing as joint heirs with Christ. Daddy God will with-hold no good thing from us. He sees us as sons and daughters... valued and validated.

Victory and Value in Brokenness

Brokenness can be a difficult experience to understand, but what if our broken pieces aren't meant to diminish us? What if they actually make us more valuable? In our lives, we often face trials, heartache, and moments of deep despair that feel like they have shattered us. Yet, when we bring these broken pieces to God, He doesn't just mend them—He transforms them, infusing us with His grace and restoring our worth in ways we never imagined. Like the ancient Japanese art of Kintsugi, where broken pottery is repaired with gold, God uses our brokenness to create something even more beautiful.

Kintsugi, meaning "**golden joinery**," is a centuries-old technique where broken pottery is repaired with lacquer mixed with powdered gold, silver, or platinum. Rather than hiding the cracks, Kintsugi highlights them, making the object even more precious than before it was broken.

In the same way, God replaces our broken pieces and refines us with Himself, making us more valuable than we were before. The gold represents His divine presence, the very essence of His character that fills our voids, heals our wounds, and restores our identity.

We often try to hide our cracks and imperfections, striving for perfection in our own strength. We cover up flaws, hoping to appear whole and without blemish. This facade is usually rooted in shame, which, over time, becomes unbearable. When we grasp our efforts to achieve perfection within ourselves, it will always be impossible. No matter how hard we try, we cannot be perfect by our own efforts. Only God can take our imperfections and create something greater than we could ever imagine. Isaiah 64:6 reminds us that "all our righteous acts are like filthy rags" when done in our own strength. Perfection within ourselves is impossible, but God's grace turns our brokenness into beauty. Acknowledging our inherent limitations and imperfections as humans brings an incredible sense of freedom.

When we face brokenness, it's easy to feel as though the damage is irreparable, that our value is diminished. Well, in God's hands, every crack... every wound... and every scar becomes a mark of redemption—a reminder of how He lovingly restores us to reflect His glory. As Paul writes in 2 Corinthians 12:9, "My grace is sufficient for you, for my power is made perfect in weakness." It is in our weakness and brokenness that God's strength and redemption shine through.

Moreover, 2 Corinthians 4:7 reminds us that we are like jars of clay holding an incredible treasure: "But we have this treasure in jars of clay to show that this all-surpassing power is from God and not from us." Though we are fragile and imperfect, we carry the treasure of God's presence, demonstrating that the power to restore, redeem, and shine comes from Him—not from our own strength.

Redemption in the Cracks

Every crack in our vessel tells a story of redemption. Just as a repaired Kintsugi bowl becomes more valuable because of its golden seams, so do our lives become more valuable through the redemption stories of our broken-ness. These cracks are not to be hidden or disguised; they are to be celebrated as part of our unique journey with God.

Each crack speaks of God's grace in the midst of pain. One crack may tell of the time we were abandoned, but God stepped in as our Comforter. Another crack may remind us of a season of loss, where God became our Provider and Restorer. Another might mark a time when we doubted our worth, only for God to remind us that we are fearfully and wonderfully made (Psalm 139:14)

In the world's eyes, cracks may be seen as flaws, but in God's eyes, they are the very places where His grace shines through. He doesn't merely patch us up; He refines us, filling our lives with His Spirit, which is far more precious than gold. These cracks, redeemed by God, become the golden seams that hold us together, making us stronger, more resilient, and more radiant with His love.

Beauty In Brokenness

Many times, we perceive ourselves through the lens of imperfection—seeing lack, hurt, betrayal, abandonment, and rejection. The enemy understands that we were born with a divine purpose and seeks to distort our self-perception. Early in life, Satan begins sowing seeds of deception and lies in our spirits, using the wounds of hurt, betrayal, and rejection to undermine our confidence in God's promises. However, what he intends for evil, God turns for our good. The story of Joseph in the Old Testament exemplifies this truth. Joseph faced rejection and betrayal at the tender age of 17, yet God, who is the Alpha and Omega, knew the end from the beginning (Read Genesis 37-50.

Genesis 50:20 AMP underscores this truth: "As for you, you meant evil against me, but God meant it for good in order to bring about this present outcome, that many people would be kept alive [as they are this day]." The emphasis on "but GOD" highlights a crucial point—victory follows every instance where God intervenes. He consistently orchestrates circumstances for our triumph. Just as God foresaw Joseph's victory from the outset, He views us through the lens of triumph.

The world often tells us that we must be perfect to be valuable, but God flips that script. Our true worth comes not from an absence of brokenness, but from the beauty that God creates out of our broken pieces. Each crack tells a story... your story. Just as Kintsugi vessels are deemed more valuable after golden repairs, the same applies to us when we allow God to work through our brokenness.

We must remember that our attempts at perfection in our own strength will always fall short. God never asks us to be flawless, only to surrender our brokenness to Him. He replaces our brokenness with His strength, fills our emptiness with His presence, and refines our character to reflect His love. The cracks are not signs of defeat but of His victory and redemption in our lives. Just as gold adorns the cracks of Kintsugi pottery, so too does God's grace adorn the broken places of our hearts, making us precious in His sight.

As 2 Corinthians 4:7 reminds us, we hold a treasure within these "jars of clay"—God's all-surpassing power, which works through our weaknesses and cracks to showcase His strength. Our brokenness reveals His glory and power, transforming weakness into strength, pain into purpose, and trials into testimonies of His redeeming love.

This profound truth of God's power shining through our brokenness is beautifully illustrated in the story of the woman at the well in John 4. Just as we, fragile jars of clay, carry His treasure within, this woman, weighed down by shame and rejection, found herself unlikely the recipient of divine validation. Her encounter with Jesus not only unveiled her past but revealed her value and purpose in His eyes. It reminds us that, no matter our cracks or imperfections, God meets us where we are, offering healing, transformation, and true validation.

Validated at the Well

I love reading about the woman at the well in John 4— her encounter with Jesus transformed her life in a profound way.

In her Well Experience, she had two significant revelations: she gained a new perspective on Jesus, and she discovered her true identity.

Encountering Christ can bring about a significant transformation in our lives. It allows us to see ourselves in a new light, the way Jesus sees us. In the presence of Jesus, the Samaritan woman was able to confront her past, her sins, and her shame. She realized that she could not continue to hold on to her old life after encountering Jesus.

With newfound clarity, she left behind her water jar, symbolizing her past, and boldly shared her '**Well Experience**' with others. She dropped her pot, her past, and her embarrassment, and shared her testimony with everyone she met. This moment marked a 'BUT GOD' situation, where the enemy's intentions failed. Her past no longer defined her; she embraced her divine purpose and stepped into her future.

"Arise [from spiritual depression to a new life], shine [be radiant with the glory and brilliance of the LORD]; for your light has come, and the glory and brilliance of the LORD has risen upon you."
(Isaiah 60:1 AMP)

The above scripture beautifully illustrates how the Samaritan woman emerged from spiritual depression into a new life, radiating the glory of the Lord. As we conclude this chapter, let's take a moment to reflect on the profound truth that an encounter with Christ can validate and empower our lives. Just like the woman at the well who found her identity and purpose in the presence of Jesus, we too can experience transformation and renewal when we encounter Him in our own lives. It is important for us to embrace the reality that we are validated and valued beyond measure by our Heavenly Father, and allow this truth to shape how we see ourselves and how we live our lives.

In the upcoming chapter, we will delve deeper into the journey of overcoming the voices of doubt, insecurity, and inadequacy that often plague our minds. I invite you to join me as we explore how understanding our inherent value and worth in Christ enables us to rise above the negative voices and walk confidently in our God-given identity.

Validation Scriptures

I am created In God's likeness.
Ephesians 4:24

I am a whole new person with a whole new life…
2 Corinthians 5:17

I am God's incredible work of art; His workmanship.
Ephesians 2:10

I am totally and completely forgiven.
1 John 1:9

I am spiritually alive.
Ephesians 2:5

I am a citizen of Heaven.
Philippians 3:20

I am God's disciple-maker.
Matthew 28:19

I am the light of the world.
Matthew 5:14

I am triumphant
2 Corinthians 2:14

I am God's child.
Galatians 3:26

Think About It:

Consider the broken areas in your life. Are you willing to let God repair and restore them with His grace? Each crack holds a story of redemption—a testament to God's transforming love and power. Just as the Kintsugi artist lovingly repairs broken pottery with gold, so too does God lovingly redeem our brokenness, making us vessels of greater worth. You are not defined by your broken-ness, but by the God who redeems it. Let Him fill your cracks with His golden grace, turning your life into a story of beauty, resilience, and divine redemption.

Reflect on how encountering Christ brings validation and empowerment to your life. Where might you need to release past shame or insecurities? Embrace your true identity as a beloved child of God. Just as the Samaritan woman at the well discovered her identity and purpose in Christ's presence, you too can allow the truth of God's unconditional love to shape how you see yourself and live your life. Take a moment to consider how Christ's transformative power can renew every part of your story.

"Our value is
not diminished
by trials —it is
revealed
through them!"

CHAPTER SEVEN
Victoriously Valuable
Beyond the Voices

Do you believe that you are valuable and victorious? Our belief system has a profound effect on our ability to live a victorious life and walk in our worth. When we attach a price tag to our worth based on our imperfections, we end up seeking approval from others instead of realizing our true value. Even though words of encouragement are great, we shouldn't use them to determine our worth.

At times, we may feel worthless and defeated, as if the very essence of who we are is called into question. The weight of rejection and failure can crush our spirits, leaving us feeling utterly discarded and hopeless. However, our value and victory are never contingent upon our circumstances or the opinions of others. God sees us as priceless treasures, worthy of love, grace, and redemption.

Our belief system significantly impacts how we see ourselves. Ultimately, it determines our ability to walk in our worth and live victoriously. We can withstand the storms of doubt and insecurity that threatens to engulf us by anchoring our identity in the unchanging truth of God's Word.

While seeking validation from others may provide temporary relief, true fulfillment comes from knowing our worth in the eyes of our Creator. We are fearfully and wonderfully made, intricately crafted by the hands of a loving God who delights in us just as we are.

Therefore, let's silence the voices of negativity and condemnation that seek to undermine our value. Instead, cultivate a belief system rooted in the unwavering truth of God's love and acceptance. By doing so, we can embrace our worth and live victoriously, knowing that we are cherished and esteemed beyond measure in the eyes of our Heavenly Father.

Silencing the Lies

We have an adversary who seeks to distort our perception of our Heavenly Father's love and esteem for us. Satan endeavors to fill our minds with lies about our identity and inheritance in Christ. His ultimate goal is to undermine our confidence in our Kingdom position and cause us to forfeit the blessings and authority we have in Christ.

To combat these attacks, we must be intentional about guarding our "thought life" and rejecting the enemy's lies. Satan knows he can never take away our position in Christ, but he will use every deceitful tactic to shake our faith and confidence. It's crucial that we engage in constant study, meditation, and declaration of God's promises to counteract the enemy's lies.

The enemy fears the day when we will boldly stand on God's promises and fully embrace our royal position as children of the King. He trembles at the thought of us walking in the authority and power that Christ has bestowed upon us. It's time for us to arise, and take our rightful place as heirs of God's Kingdom.

Remember, you are called, you are chosen, and you are royal. Embrace your identity as a daughter of the King, a member of the royal priesthood, and God's masterpiece. Rise up, declare your position, and walk confidently in the authority that is yours in Christ.

Royal and Worth It

Do you grasp the full extent of your royal identity in Christ? It is the source of a purposeful and hopeful life. This transformative truth not only empowers us but also ignites a fire within us, inspiring us to reach for our full potential. For many years, I found myself praying aimlessly, unaware of the posture I should take and settling for less than my inheritance. I needed more spiritual wisdom to fully grasp the legacy I had inherited.

Through my own journey, I've learned that I am not defined by temptations or imperfections. As scripture tells us, if any man or woman is "in Christ," they are made new. This unveiling has not only liberated me but also filled me with a sense of relief and hope, transforming my life.

Being a child... an heir of the King transcends age, ethnicity, or family background; it is solely rooted in God's amazing grace. This realization has freed me from the burden of trying to earn my worth and allowed me to embrace the truth that my identity is secure in Christ.

As believers, we have been granted access to everything God has promised us, but it is essential to approach Him with the correct posture when making our requests known. In 2 Corinthians 1:21-22, God expresses how valuable we are to Him and the rights attached to our worth. Our approach to Him reflects our trust in His promises. Have you ever found yourself praying from a place of unworthiness? Do you trust man's abilities more than God's authority?

Consider the Canaanite woman whose daughter was severely ill and demon-possessed. Despite societal norms that deemed it unacceptable for a woman to approach a man, especially Jesus, she was unwavering in her pursuit of her daughter's deliverance. In her desperation, she approached Jesus directly, demonstrating her complete trust in Him. I resonate deeply with her desperation, as I would do anything for my own children if they were in danger or suffering. This unwavering love and concern that our Heavenly Father has for us led Him to send His only Son for our rescue. He deemed us worth it.

Reflecting on the story of the Canaanite woman, we witness the unwavering faith and persistence she displayed in approaching Jesus for her daughter's healing. Her example serves as a powerful reminder of the depth of God's love and His willingness to go to great lengths for our sake. Just as the Canaanite woman trusted in Jesus for her daughter's deliverance, so too can we trust in God's promises and our identity in Christ.

This narrative highlights the importance of acknowledging our true identity as believers and reveals the depth of God's love and the lengths He is willing to go to for our sake. When we recognize ourselves as sons and daughters of God, we can approach God with confidence, knowing that we are valued and loved beyond measure. Embracing this identity empowers us to boldly claim the promises He has for us and walk in the fullness of His blessings.

Never Changing Father

The love and support of our Heavenly Father is un-wavering and constant, like having the ultimate cheerleader in our corner. Just as cheerleaders stand by their team through every victory and defeat, our Father never wavers in His commitment to us. Even when we feel like we're losing the game of life, He remains steadfast, always ready to encourage us.

Amid our struggles and shortcomings, God cheers us on and reminds us of our identity as overcomers, conquerors, and victors. His voice echoes through the challenges, urging us to keep pressing forward, knowing that He is always by our side.

No matter how far we may stray or stumble, our Father remains steadfast in His support, always ready to guide us back onto the path of righteousness. He sees the bigger picture and knows how to orchestrate every circumstance for our ultimate good.

With God as our never-changing Father, we can take heart knowing that His love for us is unwavering and His faithfulness knows no bounds. As we face the trials and tribulations of life... let's hold fast to the TRUTH! We are cherished and celebrated by the greatest cheerleader of all... our good, good **Father**.

And we know [with great confidence] that God [who is deeply concerned about us] causes all things to work together [as a plan] for good for those who love God, to those who are called according to His plan and purpose.
Romans 8:28 (AMP)

As we journey through life, we find comfort and assurance in Father God's omniscience and all-knowing nature. He is the Alpha and Omega, which means He sees our entire lives from beginning to end, including every twist and turn we will experience. His divine perspective enables Him to lead us to victory, no matter the circumstances we face.

Scripture teaches us that victory is not just a possibility but a promise to those who trust in God. Even when we are faced with difficult circumstances and feel defeated, we can hold on to the assurance that God's plans for us are good and will give us hope and a future.

When we align our perception of ourselves with the Father's perspective, we can unlock the fullness of His promises in our lives. Embracing our identity as cherished children of God, we can step into the abundant life He has prepared for us. So, let me ask you this: How do you see yourself in the eyes of your Heavenly Father?

> *But you are a chosen people, a royal priesthood,*
> *a holy nation, God's special possession,*
> *that you may declare the praises of him*
> *who called you out of darkness into his wonderful light.*
> *1 Peter 2:9(NIV)*

..And God Has Not Changed His Mind!!

As we come to the end of this journey, I want to remind you of the amazing truth you have discovered throughout this book. You are valuable, royal, and worth it in the eyes of your Heavenly Father. Throughout each chapter, we have explored the depths of God's love for us and the immeasurable worth He has placed upon us. We are not defined by our past mistakes or present circumstances but by the unchanging truth of who we are in Christ.

Take a moment to reflect on your journey to uncover this truth. Remember the moments of revelation, the challenges you have overcome, and the victories you have won. Each step has brought you closer to fully embracing your identity as a cherished child of the King.

As you move forward from this book, I encourage you to carry this truth with you in every aspect of your life. Let it shape how you see yourself, how you interact with others, and how you approach the challenges that lie ahead.

You are valuable beyond measure, royal in your inheritance, and worth every ounce of love and grace that God has bestowed upon you. May you walk in the confidence of your identity, knowing that God has not changed His mind about you, and His love for you remains constant and unwavering. May the truth of your identity continue to transform your life and illuminate the path ahead like a kingdom jewel.

-

Think About It:

As we come to the end of our journey, let us pause for a moment to ponder on the profound truth we have encountered. Do you genuinely believe that you have worth and are victorious in the eyes of God?

Consider how your belief system shapes your perception of yourself and ultimately determines your ability to embrace your self-worth and live victoriously. Are there areas where you find it challenging to fully accept yourself as a cherished child of God? Take time to reflect on how you can anchor your identity in the unchanging truth of God's Word and silence the voices of negativity and condemnation.

"True worth
is not determined
by
our condition;
it's determined
by
our God-appointed
position."

CHAPTER EIGHT
A Kingdom Jewel-
"Identified as Valuable"

In today's world, we are flooded with opinions on how we should appear and live our lives through social media. This constant influx of unsolicited advice often leads to feelings of inadequacy. It's astonishing how people readily accept the advice of strangers they've never met yet hesitate to embrace the teachings of God. Each person is uniquely created with a divine purpose and significance. You are not just a mere creation; you are a masterpiece, treasured in the eyes of God.

Psalms 8:5 proclaims, "You have made them a little lower than the angels and crowned them with glory and honor." Why is it hard to embrace the truth of our worth and identity and draw inspiration from God's Word? Well, I'm glad you asked. Basically... opinions and advice from people are tangible and immediate. We see and hear them directly. In contrast, God's Word requires faith and a relationship with the unseen. We have to put in the work. This is why it is sometimes challenging for some to trust in what is not immediately visible or audible, being that we often judge ourselves and others by what we see as opposed to what God says.

The Divine Craftsmanship

Imagine a jeweler meticulously working on a precious gem, cutting and polishing it until it reflects the perfect radiance. Similarly, God, our Master Jeweler, has crafted you with unparalleled precision and love. He has endowed you with inherent worth and a unique purpose that no one else can fulfill.

Psalm 8:5 serves as a powerful reminder of our exalted status in God's creation. The verse declares that in the eyes of the Father, we were created a little lower than the angels and crowned with glory and honor. This is not just a poetic expression but a divine truth about our identity. You are not ordinary—you are extraordinary. You were uniquely created with a divine spark that reflects the glory of the **Creator**.

Recognizing Your Worth

In a world that often places importance on material success and external appearances, it is crucial to anchor our sense of worth in God's truth. While society may value achievements, looks, and possessions, God sees beyond the surface and looks at the heart. He recognizes the intrinsic beauty within you and sees you as a precious jewel in His kingdom. This contrast between worldly standards and God's truth can be enlightening and empowering, helping us to see our true worth.

Take a moment to reflect on the fact that you are created with purpose and dignity by the CREATOR. You have been infused with extraordinary worth that is not based on external achievements or appearances. This reality means that, regardless of societal norms, your value remains constant and unwavering. When you truly internalize this truth, it can profoundly transform how you view yourself and how you engage with others and how you respond amid adversity.

Consider this: God placed His worth and value upon you before the foundations of the earth. Long before you took your first breath, He knew you and intricately wove together every detail of your being. You are not just a name in a sea of faces—He calls you by name, affirming your unique identity and significance. When He looks at you, He doesn't see a collection of random traits or talents; He sees the masterpiece He has intentionally crafted for a specific purpose. You were created with a plan in mind, each feature and gift designed with precision and love. This personal touch in your creation reveals how deeply valued and cherished you are. You are not an accident or an afterthought but a beloved creation, fashioned by the hands of the Almighty for a purpose that only you can fulfill.

Living as a Kingdom Jewel

Understanding your worth as a kingdom jewel comes with a responsibility to live in a manner that reflects your divine identity. Here are some ways to embody this truth:

-Embrace Your Unique Purpose:

Each jewel has a distinct cut and clarity, contributing to its uniqueness. Similarly, you have a specific purpose that God has designed for you. Seek to understand and fulfill this purpose with passion and dedication.

-Radiate God's Glory:

Just as a jewel shines brightly when light passes through it, let God's light shine through you. Your actions, words, and demeanor should reflect His love, grace, and truth. Be a beacon of hope and encouragement to those around you.

-Honor Your Value:

Treat yourself with the respect and dignity that a kingdom jewel deserves. This includes taking care of your physical, emotional, and spiritual well-being. Make choices that align with your divine worth and avoid situations that devalue or harm you.

-Uplift Others:

Recognize that every person you encounter is also a kingdom jewel. Encourage and uplift others, helping them to see their own worth and potential. In doing so, you create a ripple effect of positivity and transformation.

The Journey Ahead

As you journey through life, always remember that you are a kingdom jewel intricately crafted by God and crowned with glory and honor. Let Psalms 8:5 be a constant reminder of your divine worth and the incredible potential that lies within you. Embrace your identity, live with purpose, and radiate the glory of God in all that you do. In doing so, you not only honor yourself but also glorify the Master Jeweler who created you.

Understand that your presence has an impact and your life is meant to reflect the light of the Creator. Whether you are walking through seasons of joy or navigating valleys of difficulty, your steadfastness in God's truth allows His glory to shine through you, like a brilliant gem reflecting the light of the sun.

Along your assigned path, seek to grow in wisdom and grace. Surround yourself with people who see your value and encourage you to live out your calling. When you live in alignment with your divine design, you honor yourself and magnify the beauty of the Master Jeweler's handiwork.

Think About It:

Consider a time when you felt undervalued or insignificant. How does the truth of Psalms 8:5 transform that perception? Reflect on the ways you can start seeing yourself through God's eyes, recognizing the glory and honor He has bestowed upon you. As you go about your daily life, think about how you can live out your identity as a kingdom jewel, making choices that reflect your divine worth and encouraging others to see their own value as well. Remember, you are more precious than any earthly gem, crafted by the hands of the Master Jeweler Himself.

JOURNAL TAKEAWAYS

_____

_____

_____

_____

_____

_____

_____

_____

_____

_____

_____

_____

_____

_____

_____

_____

_____

_____

_____

_____

JOURNAL TAKEAWAYS

_____

_____

_____

_____

_____

_____

_____

_____

_____

_____

_____

_____

_____

_____

_____

_____

_____

_____

_____

_____

JOURNAL TAKEAWAYS

CONCLUSION

As we come to the heartfelt conclusion of our journey together in "Identified As Valuable: Royal & Worth It," I want to encourage you to take a moment to reflect on the profound truths you've discovered in this book. The journey has been about discovering, healing, empowering ourselves, and understanding the depth of God's love for us and the immeasurable worth He has placed upon us.

In this time of significant identity issues and the common phrase "I identify as," I am convinced that knowing our worth and value according to our heavenly DNA is the key to living and seeing ourselves as VALUABLE. This understanding is more than just a concept; it is a transformative realization that shapes how we live, think, and perceive our place in the world.

Think of it this way: Just as a diamond's value is not determined by external factors but by its inherent qualities, our value is intrinsic, rooted in our creation by God. Society's labels and standards can often cloud our vision, making us question our worth. However, the Bible, like a manufacturer's manual, provides clarity and truth. It reminds us that we are fearfully and wonderfully made, created with a purpose and endowed with inherent worth and value.

Throughout the pages of this book, we've embarked on a journey to peel away the layers of doubt, fear, and insecurity. We've explored the profound truths of our divine identity and the love that God has lavished upon us. This revelation is not just enlightening; it is empowering. It calls us to rise above the noise of societal judgments and to embrace our God-given identity with confidence and grace.

During moments of peaceful reflection, it's important to recall the times when you've had breakthroughs or epiphanies, and also when you've faced obstacles but managed to overcome them. These experiences have helped you grow and mature as an individual, bringing you closer to fully embracing your unique identity as a beloved child of the King. So, take some time to appreciate the progress you've made and recognize that each step you've taken has contributed to your personal growth and development.

When we understand and embrace our worth, we unlock our full potential. We begin to live in alignment with God's divine plan, experiencing the fullness of life that He intended for us. This journey is not without its challenges, but it is one that leads to profound joy, peace, and fulfillment.

May you walk forward in the confidence of your identity, knowing that God has not changed His mind about you, and His love for you remains constant and unwavering. May the truth of your identity, explored in "Identified As Valuable: Royal and Worth It," continue to transform your life, illuminate the path ahead, and inspire others to discover their own worth and value in Christ.

As we come to the end of our time together, I want to encourage you to hold firmly to these truths. Let them take root in your heart and mind. Remember, your worth is not defined by the world, but by the **Creator** who formed you. Embrace your unique identity as a cherished child of God— royal and one-of-a-kind and allow this realization to transform every aspect of your life.

Your value does not shield you from challenges or hardships. However, it assures you that the One who calls you precious will walk with you through every trial. His presence is not just a promise, it's a reality, and nothing can separate you from His unwavering love.

You are significant beyond measure, and your life reflects God's extraordinary love and purpose. You are treasured. You are irreplaceable. You are uniquely crafted and deeply adored by your Heavenly Father.

Your worth is immeasurable, and your significance is undeniable.

JOURNAL TAKEAWAYS

_____

_____

_____

_____

_____

_____

_____

_____

_____

_____

_____

_____

_____

_____

_____

_____

_____

_____

_____

JOURNAL TAKEAWAYS

JOURNAL TAKEAWAYS

JOURNAL TAKEAWAYS

_____

_____

_____

_____

_____

_____

_____

_____

_____

_____

_____

_____

_____

_____

_____

_____

_____

_____

_____

ABOUT THE AUTHOR

Renee Minor Johnson is a wife (of an Army Veteran), published Author, Empowerment Speaker/Coach, and Minister. Her God-given gifts of speaking and writing have given her opportunities to share a message of hope in traditional and non-traditional settings. She believes we should use every God-given "gift" to glorify God and build His Kingdom.

Her writing and publishing of books unveil her inspiring testimonial message of "hopeful expectation." Her Christian faith is the foundation of all of her writing. The core of her message is how our worth, true identity, and God-given purpose are divinely connected. Renee is convinced that holding true to our identity in Christ empowers us to live forward (meaning leaving the past behind). Her books speak to her passion for seeing true transformation in the lives of "hope-loss" people.

Renee is the CEO of ChampionsWithin Kingdom Builders and the Founder of the Reigning Royalty Empowerment & Mentorship Academy. The foundational mission of both organizations is to infuse hope, renew minds, and transform lives by tapping into the most authentic version of whom we were created to become.

Renee has written and published multiple books (including prayer journals and devotionals). She describes her third book, "Ashamed No More," as the roadmap of her testimonial journey from a "hope-loss" place to a "hope-infused" space. Renee says, "Being affected by our past is understandable, but being defined by our history is unacceptable. We are not what we did nor what happened to us. We are who God called us... fearfully and wonderfully made. She attributes this revelation to her growing faith, and she passionately shares this faith-filled message with everyone she meets.

REFERENCES

Note: The translations used for most scriptures are as marked; KJV used otherwise. (**The Holy Bible... AMP, GW, MSG, NLT, NIV**)

Royalty/That's How He Sees Me:
Renee M. Johnson

Thinking for a Change:
John C. Maxwell

A Jewel in His Crown:
Priscilla Shirer

His Princess/Love Letters From Your King:
Sheri R. Shepherd